Beyond
A
Master

Beyond
A
Master

Denise R. Cooney

AMETHYST BOOKS
NEW YORK   LONDON

Published in the United States by Amethyst Books, 160 West 71st Street, Apt. 17D, New York, N.Y. 10023 and in the United Kingdom by Amethyst Books, 44 Gledstanes Road, London W14.

Designed by Paperweight.

Library of Congress Catalog Card Number: 87-072726.

ISBN 0–944256–01–5.

Amethyst Books are distributed in the United States by Publishers Group West, Emeryville, Ca. and in the United Kingdom by Gateway Books, Bath.

Dedication

I want to thank my mom, Rich C., my dad, Joan Grigsby, Sister Thedra, Janet Neal, Maureen O'Brian, Leslie Caren, Fran Peragine, Kathy Trier, David Carroll, Matthew Mingle, Meher Baba, Marcy Williams and Peter Hefter, and most of all GOD for showing me that faith, patience and love are the keys to the Universe.

Contents

Introduction

I am an individual who, like anyone else, has their days of ups and down. I have been studyingspirituality since 1965. I have been to India, lived in England and moved to California. While in all these places, I kept looking for that hidden mystery. Then, one day, my guides told me to move back to New Jersey – a highly unlikely place to find yourself, but, then again, what do I know? So, in my daily travels, I have been channeling for the past ten years, teaching people how to work with their own energy and working with the movement of light. And, I might add, in the process I have been learning about my own TEACHER WITHIN.

Then for some unknown reason, my guides instructed me to go into the Paramedic Program. How dare they, I thought. I want to do spiritual healing. You know, sometimes I can get so closed-minded and think that "spirit" just means "esoteric"! I now understand that the Program has opened me up to see the human body in a very spiritual way.

What I am saying is that listening to your voice is

indeed the process. I couldn't believe that I would actually be putting a book together, but, then, it isn't me, it is truly spirit. I feel that there are many good people out there letting the voice speak through them. But, more important is that you make up your own mind about your need to accept. I want you to know that TRUTH is in the mind of the BEHOLDER. If there is anything that you don't agree with, that is fine with me. The purpose of this manuscript is to hopefully shed light on your situation. I hope you enjoy this and see your growth.

Everyday, with increasing interest, I watch the world and the progress we are all seemingly making on our evolution of self. Sometimes, I am not sure whether we are really focused in on the big picture – the everyday comings and goings of our personal lives often make it all feel so overwhelming. Sometimes, when we become too reflective, we cannot escape our own crossfire.

There are days where sacred wisdom, words of encouragement and practices of meditation and spirituality can leave you flat. They are usually on days when you need it the most. The ego, the ten per cent personality self thrives on separation from God.

When working on the path and trying to "see" the

overall scheme of things, life can seem to start feeling claustrophobic at these times. Feelings of unworthiness and a scrambling for "what is truly mine?"

You for the most part can spend your time pacing, cleaning the house, listening to music, calling up your friends – usually people spend all types of time doing everything except sitting and listening and letting the emotion come up.

Granted, it can be very uncomfortable indeed to deal with the very thing that is making you squirm but so what? Maybe for once you will be able to identify it and then (imagine!) you might actually overcome it – right there or over a period of time. But the main point here is that it can take some courage to be able to see it. The cause could lie simple and easy like some unrelinquished childhood fear set by our parents or, more intensely, by our incorrect choice of partner, lifestyle, etc.

Many people are content enough to just squirm and say, "Oh, I'll get over it soon enough", and go out and belt a few drinks, take some drugs, see the movies, etc., "until it goes away". Unfortunately, it doesn't go away; it can come out in nervousness, pain in the body, headaches, nightmares, mood swings, etc. Now why would "God" have all of this happen to you? This is just the point. God gives you freedom of choice. It's just not enough to say you forgive. You need to see what you are releasing. What is important here is learning to identify and cope with our feelings.

In the physical plane, things are modernizing at a phenomenal rate, but human nature remains at the same rate basically from the inception of the human form. Never before have so many techniques and modalities been available to man: Mysteries revealed, truths explained, miracles manifesting, Christ's new name revealed. Yet, still, even among this cloud rushing in to bring forth renewed life into the consciousness of mankind, people still want instant healings for age old problems when the answers have been revealed for centuries. In order to truly understand God we must first understand ourselves.

When on the path, the painstaking effort to know oneself and to be able to learn and act accordingly becomes clear and then sometimes fades from view. It is really clear when you are joy filled and really dim when you need to exercise it the most.

Why this fluctuation of the emotion?

Remember the human form is truly one of the hardest forms to create and sustain balance. Remember to have complete balance is what inertly all of humanity is striving for. But also remember that the ego strives to keep the world of illusion, maya, false reality alive and everytime you get closer to God and try to truly practice what you preach, it will make you move and shut down and feel the separation from God and *this alone* is truly the source of all of humanity's problems on life, success, love, peace and prosperity.

We are saying it is that simple. People always want to be right. So they scream from the rooftops, try to convince – neighbors, relatives, friends – that they have been wronged. Sometimes not looking at the source of their misfortune may be as simple.

Why wallow in a sea of despair when what is needed is the rescue? The rescue means following our heart even in the face of adversity, even when it means changing our lifestyles. Sometimes it is hard to humble ourselves, to admit we are wrong, to feel ourselves stripped of our defences, our walls that protect the strong yet very fragile ego.

We clamor more and more and seemingly get less and less until there is final surrender and what a feeling it is! Total humility, total love, total selflessness. A feeling that can bring us to our knees. It can bring us to our emotional unwinding. Total trust. For this is the moment where you can be cut down to the core and annihilated to give and open so fully that you see how insignificant any large problem is. It is made out of papier mache compared to the fabric of eternal life.

So where then comes in the balance? People say don't go too deep, yet the truth is we don't go deep enough to truly face our problems. We don't stand firmly in the land of the shadow of the unknown, willing to slay words, thoughts and ideals that no longer serve the highest purpose. Countries do this for years. Political ideologies clash. Parents and children rebel. Religious beliefs conflict.

Everyone wants to be right at the cost sometimes of human life. This is humanity lost in the realm of the shadow. When light moves in, the shadow changes and sometimes moves behind you, but when you face the invisible, the ever-changing, and see that you truly have the power to remould it, then you can release it.

In learning about ourselves we must also learn to accept ourselves – see the lesson and let ourselves learn to deal with life's little challenges in a new way, every time handling it a little differently, every time handling it with a bit more care, every time acknowledging we won't fall back into outmoded, outdated ways of handling life.

How does God fit in in all of this?

It is the discovery of mastery, first of yourself; of being in charge of your emotions, not forcing them but watching them and working out your feelings so you express yourself clearly; seeing that if you please everyone else then you are not honoring the God in you who wants to come out.

How can one have clear communication with the higher self if the lower self is confused and afraid of its own shadow?

Bravery is called for on the Path. Jesus Christ has shown us in countless examples how courage must be displayed. Even in his life, his emotions sometimes got in the way, but the Christ in him prevailed.

Even he had a hard time in the physical body. He was open to all types of situations and made his human qualities like an open book to the whole world. So, why are we so ashamed of the fact that, while studying the law of spirit, we will all make mistakes?

You realize that there are a lot of texts about spirituality in the "New Age". Very few seem to really address what to do when you have applied all the affirmations and visualizations and still are not making any headway. Doesn't it sometimes make you feel stupid that all these other people seem to have just found their perfect partner and are fully employed with perfect health, while you are just trying to get out of bed to look what is in store for you at the office?

I am not saying that these books are not inspirational; I am just stating that sometimes when things aren't going your way, it isn't always because of some personal limitation you have. Sometimes, it can be the darkside of your personality really putting you to the test to see how strong your belief system is.

Am I insinuating the darkside exists? Well, frankly, yes! This is an issue that seems to be shoved under the proverbial rug with the "New Age Set". A few years ago, I did not believe in anything but the power of God as taught to me by someone else. I was told that, if I just believed in the strength of the gold or white light, I would be protected! Ha! Ha! Spirituality is not all brown rice and roses.

We are working with unlocking ancient information that has been shared from adept to teacher for centuries. This power is very strong indeed. It allowed Christ to raise the dead. Nowadays, everyone and their mother can read in a book how to channel, do healings and more. The "New Age" Movement has become a very dangerous, simplistic do-it-yourself booby trap. The energy we are talking about is God and, on a human plane, other powerful energies that have been stored up in the conscious memory of man throughout the ages.

How did the Truth taught by Jesus Christ get received by the masses? In fear and misunderstanding for the most part – so he was crucified.

In like manner, our emotions may truly rebel at

seeing the power available, of the eternal love and divine order that is possible. Our emotions may try to kill the Christ within us by providing incredibly hard situations for us to overcome.

But the more light of God's love you can draw from, the quicker the energy of the darkness is rendered harmless.

Then, truly, the balance is one of constant work. It is not completed in one meditation or one thousand. It is finished when you become a Master. It can take lifetimes. But you must start somewhere and realize that you have many parts like God has many expressions and, like God, you are one with all of Divine Consciousness.

So how does one hold on in focusing in on God? By finding a teacher or a Master (if you are so fortunate) and stay with them, follow and obey their instructions until you feel your connection with God.

Remember, teachers can only take you to the same place, plane or level where they are, so don't ever become too dependent. They can guide you, help you release Karma, *but never* do they replace *God*. If you blindly believe every word, then look at your dependency and learn to become independent, for God is the main focus.

Techniques are not what is being shared right now,

but learning to cultivate the soul for receiving Love and releasing age-old bonds of slavery.

So, what is the strongest element in the Universe? It is not anything you or I can touch. It is something that sometimes we feel, never anything that we can fully understand. It is only something that we can experience.

Love is the strongest element in the whole of God's creation. It is a very healing vibration, and, while in human relationships, we can begin to understand, on a relating level, our connection with God. Even now, as I write, I am experiencing the whole spectrum of that feeling. Love, when it is in our lives on a personal level, makes us glow. People, friends and relatives tell us how we are filled with a light that has total radiance. Then, when a relationship changes on a human level, we experience a whole gamut of feelings on the other end of the spectrum: total isolation, despair, heartbreak.

You are free to create any world that you wish. You are free to believe any way that you want. You are free to have any lifestyle that you feel is yours. It's all a matter of belief in God.

So how do we contact that God Spirit? Tap into that love. When you are *looking* for a sign you'll probably miss it. Just stay open, enjoy a child's voice. Look at life around you. Clean up your environment. Work on your physical body. Sing from your heart. Find something good in yourself. And make peace with your enemies. Make peace with your enemies, whether they are real or imaginary. Do not let yourself be separated from God due to hatred. People can die from lack of love – broken hearts, etc. And consistent hatred can make a person become ill inside and create cancer, etc. Please realize you are capable of healing all your ills quickly and permanently with LOVE. Anger and resentment can bring poverty in all areas of your life. Why allow this to happen? So are we saying your feelings are wrong? NO! We are saying let your feelings come up, identify them and then release and let go and create a vacuum so that love can come in its place.

In the Beginning . . .

This is to introduce you to the concept of Sananda and Sanat Kumara. I was first introduced myself by Sister Thedra from Mount Shasta, California. She is a channel of many years with many experiences all of her own.

At first I was channeling my own guide ASHTAR, then after a while the concept of channeling a Master or two wasn't out of the question.

Now let's address the nature of channeling as it applies to all channels around the world. First, you must understand that anyone who has the capability to do this type of work isn't always the most spiritually evolved person. Their experiences in life aren't any different than your own. We are all channels to some degree or another. We have all had moments of saying, "Oh now if I would have only listened to myself." This is what is known as being open to your higher self. So it is on that rare occasion that we let ourselves listen to ourselves and we find that we are O.K. after all.

Now about that channeling process and Sananda.

Again, let me emphasize for you what I, the channel, am all about. During the process of this type of work I have found many people who claim very outrageous things. First of all, there are no pure channels anywhere in the world today. If they were as they claim, pure channels, then, in fact, they would be Masters. How, you may ask, is that so? Well, I will tell you from my own limited point of view. As a channel myself, I know that as the guides come through me they have a lot of rough material to work through. My own personality, for one, and the limitation that is presented by my own lack of belief in some form or another. Now, I am not saying that I am a wimpy person all confused all the time and shivering with apprehension every time I am about to channel. No, what I am saying is that they have me, Denise R. Cooney, that they have to come through. No matter how clear I am, they still must come through me. Now, another thing about this channeling business.

Why would Masters present themselves in full through just one medium or channel? Think about that for a while. The Master energy is so overwhelming that for it to come through one individual would wipe them out, literally. Now, let me go over that with you. If I say I am channeling the Christ energy, with all of the power that is behind that energy, wouldn't you imagine that I would have to be quite prepared spiritually as well as physically to accept that energy? The answer to a question such as that is, "yes". But why would a Master, with all of the available resources and power and manifestation capabilities have to come through a human being such as myself?

The answer, as far as I can gather it, is that only a portion of that Christ consciousness is coming through me. And another portion through someone else. That is what the messengers are really all about. Not to be adorned or be admired. They are just plain old messengers for their boss.

And, as open as the person is, so is the information. Now, I am working on the path just like everyone else. I am working on relationships and how to live my life in a balanced form, just like you are. Sure, I can hear myself and my guides all the time. But that doesn't mean I always listen to what is being said. I have free will just like everyone else. Now, let's address another issue about channeling.

You have free will all the time. If someone is channeling a guide like Sambula or some other wild-named guide, you don't have to blindly follow what they say just because Sambula said it.

I have noticed that during this time people are getting incredibly hung up and are hanging onto every

✠

23

word of some of these disincarnate beings. Just because I channel or someone else does, it is to be utilized as an adjunct to your growth if it suits your Truth. Just because a guide claims to be some ancient something or other, don't go losing yourself in this.

We live in very dangerous times, so to speak. Remember the words of Christ. He basically said at the time when the world would change many would come in His name, but He would know them not and that even the elect would be fooled.

Disincarnate beings may be powerful, but they aren't always spiritual. Some of the things that are being put out now about spirituality are very discouraging to me. You know it doesn't matter what you eat or drink or wear to be spiritual. It doesn't even matter what teacher you have been learning from. What does matter is that you see even the so-called "unenlightened" group of humanity and realize for yourself that they too are God.

Don't let this so-called New Age movement become a real isolationist type of movement. What is the difference if you are a follower of Meher Baba or Christ or Krishna or whatever? Don't become elitist and think because you know of a channel who is famous you are better off than those who don't. If you allow yourself to get into that, you become trapped.

☩

Also, as far as responsibility goes, remember to take charge of your life – don't just follow. Don't shrug and say, "Oh, I guess it wasn't meant to be." Oh, yick, I have heard that so much when people don't follow up on their obligations. What would have happened to us if our parents or employers didn't take care of us the way they should have? Could you imagine a payday coming and the Accounting Department decided that their own personal problems were just so overwhelming that they decided to shrug off that payday? Their excuse for you not getting paid is, "Oh, I guess it wasn't meant to be." If there is responsibility in your life, accept it. Pay attention to it. Be happy that you have asked for it in the first place.

Now back to this material that I have put out.

Who is Sananda? This information about Sananda is channeled information. I have heard the name from Sister Thedra and from the lessons of the Association of Sananda and Sanat Kumara in Mount Shasta, California. When I started channeling Sananda, at first I felt reluctant to tell anyone. I felt that only Sister or someone much better than myself was qualified to really be bringing in a force of this magnitude.

I will allow Sananda to introduce himself to you. For I feel that my description of who I think he is may not do him justice.

Sananda Speaks

Greeting dear ones. On this day I thank you for allowing me to come through your being once again. I will let you know that I am the new name for the CHRIST. Do you find this unreasonable? What does it matter to one such as yourself if I come in as Christ or Sananda? I have said I will come again with a new name. It is now time for the movement of the Christ force to come into play into the very main fabric of your daily lives. All too many warnings have been given to your Planet about the changes of the spiritual force and that the levels of consciousness are truly starting to shift and change. All you have to do is to watch your mundane news to see that the shifting of the planetary consciousness is in full swing. You will be having more natural type disasters and more of your nuclear accidents. People will be forced to remove the veil of ignorance of separation. You will have to come to the aid of one another or truly your planet will not be able to handle the force that will be unleashed.

I have not come to start a new religion but, rather, to awaken you to the Truth that you are all of one mind. You have heard the words of mine before. Many of you are starting to awaken to those words only two thousand years after I have spoken them. You must understand that over the last few holiday seasons, as you have called them, we, the Masters of your consciousness, have been gathering together over many of your physical spiritual power points and have been narrowing down the veil between the world of illusion that you call life and the doorway to eternity.

Once approximately every seven hundred years we come together to bring into the Earth part of the Divine Plan. Only now all of the pieces are ready for understanding. We will be in physical form for those of you that can truly see. Not only will we be with you through your meditations but we will also be talking through many of what you call channels. Soon there will come the day that the use for channels will be unnecessary due to the fact that you will be in touch with that planetary logos that you call the higher self. All that speaks of my name is not of the highest quality. I must tell you that the dark side or the world that some of you have called evil is also gaining in energy and power for it knows instinctively that its time is coming to an end. Please, for your sake, not for the sake of God, be aware that all that says it is spiritual is not necessarily so. *Be Aware.* For the time is quickly coming that you will be called upon to choose your weapons so to speak. Follow your hearts. Listen to the *Christ Within*. You must see that, when it comes to battling fears and limitations, empty words that you call prayers will have no holding power over this energy as it tries to make its last stand before the veil is lifted. What is called for here is an *unswerving Faith and Trust and Love of God* – not the empty type of childishness that some of you display. No amount of crystals or other objects that you call power will be there to protect you. You are the crystal, you are the living prayer. Do not think for one moment that it is just in meditation that your strength and energy come through.

It is through your every action and all of your words and thoughts that you will show who you are. Your eating habits are of no recourse for us. But the way that you eat your energy and the way that you spread your love is very important.

There is no more time left for beating around the bush. You must decide. I will not be with the faint-hearted or those who are hot then cold. I will be with those whose faith and trust is there from the very marrow of the bone. This is my planet; the world is entrusted to me to work the energy through. I work with Buddha and Krishna to work the energy through all of you.

I understand that many of you are interested in extraterrestrials. Has it not occurred to you that you too are of the same breed? Do you think that the Earth is on a shelf somewhere in someone's closet? No, it is also in Space somewhere in the Universe. You too are from outer space. The Federation of the Brotherhoods is waiting for this moment in time to work with the Earth and the inhabitants to gain in structure the growing consciousness of the God-like mind. Do you think that the God mind does not still grow in understanding who the I AM is? As you grow in awareness, so does that small portion of the Creator as you call it. I am your Brother. I am what you are. You are within me, and I am within you. I have put out my words of truth through many.

Yet there are many who make a mockery of the *Truth*. They do not warn you of the dangers of the spiritual path. They teach you techniques yet they know not themselves how to work with the energy. They would rather have you think that prosperity means some little game to become rich. They would have you think that the spiritual path is a rosy lily white path with no consequence of working with very powerful energy.

Do you not understand that this is how ignorance or

evil as you call it keeps pulling down the veil over your eyes? Anyone can learn a skill and perform magical tricks as you call them. Be aware that all healings do not come from spirit. They do come from the world of forms. You are working with binding Karma at that point. Do you not realize that some people have the disease process to work out their Karma? You will not play *God* in trying to change their course of destiny or you will pay the price for that work. If this is making you feel uncomfortable, *Good*. I am forgiveness. But I will not let my family be lulled into a false sense of security about the spiritual path.

I am not of anger. I am not of fear. I must tell you that in a way there is a type of battle going on. You must awaken from your sleep. You must awaken now. The American Indians as you call them have been aware of the *Dark Side* as they call it. Your major religions have called it by many names, yet they do not really fully understand the concept.

This is not a game. You must allow yourself to always ask, is this for my higher good and good of all concerned? It is very easy to get wrapped up in the ego and think that working with the *Light* as you so call it will be the only protection that you need. You must understand that many of you look to us as children walking around in adult clothing. Grow

31

up, wake up, take full responsibility for your lives.

Many of you are using creative visualizations for techniques. Many of you are really trying to force your will upon others. Be aware if you are truly visualizing for your highest and best good or if you are trying to manipulate the universe. Herein lies the rub. Then you are working with the Black Brotherhood. I will not let you sleep any more until you address these questions.

I want you to stop being like my sheep who are straying too far from the fold. Be aware that many will come as wolves in sheep's clothing. I have sent you the warning for hundreds of years. When will you listen?

Understand that Light itself does illuminate, but it also opens up the gateway for other energies to see who you are, and if you are not prepared, they will play with you. I am not trying to say that working with energy is wrong; you must understand it is powerful and one weekend class on opening to your awareness is a very dangerous game indeed.

Knowledge does take a millisecond to enter and sometimes many years to absorb for understanding. Granted, the awareness of the *Now* is growing faster and faster. Just be aware of the other things that are out there.

Many of my teachers are being lulled to sleep. Many of my family members are being taken over by beings that say they do not have to come in human form. They do not wish to make the same mistake as me. Is this talk of some being who is spiritual or who is guided by wisdom? Listen carefully. These beings are just guests coming to someone else's home. If they start destroying the channel, then are they truly beings of wisdom? Who are they, then? Just some disincarnate beings with limited knowledge and some of the dark side. *Be aware . . . be aware. . . .* We live in very dangerous times, so to speak, and at the same time you are living in a time that is filled with overwhelming joy. But remember that birth can be a painful process. *I love you and will protect you, but you must truly be open to the laws.* God speaks to all, but all do not speak of God. *Be aware.*

Sanat Kumara Speaks

I am the one known as the master and lord of this part of your Universe. I work with the Christ or Sananda as his new vibration is called. Many of you know me by the names of the mystery schools. It is my energy that has sustained it so far. I have come in hope that you, the children of the third planet from the sun called earth, will hear the call. You have been told that you are going into a heart chakra vibration.

You are also moving out of the third chakra, which is the power center for manipulation and the end expression of the limitation of man. It is no wonder that many of you are now fascinated with the wonders of the three-ring circus of the occult. Move onward and out of the expression of these ways. You must understand the conditions of the heart and what love means, for this is the only energy that will protect you through the changes. Many of you will die from disease and from man-made type diseases, yet many of you will live through these changes and will still not learn. I say if you find yourself past the first series of tests and still have not learned, then truly, as they say in the bible, "Woe to the inhabitants of the Earth". Truly you will ask to die and it will not come. When the energies are dividing up the planet and the forces of the one known to you all as GOD comes to manifest not in allegorical terms as you all seem to assume but literally, you will feel as if an energy more powerful than the sun has come to burn you away. Work now not on skills of levitations or manifestation but faith. Then all that you need and ask for will be provided not by being obedient little puppies but truly servants of the one most HIGH! I am here to tell you of the change of things and to help you through the change. As the *Christ* has announced, it is not for the weak of heart but for those who are willing to risk family, friends and your very life itself, if need be, to raise the consciousness of this earth. What are you so afraid of death for, you people of the supposed New Age? I say there is no New Age, just a releasing of the eternal Now upon your Earth. As the wave of energy goes from Galaxy to Galaxy you will be able to hear the symphony of angels. Not the sounds of the astral planes that you call music today. I am not saying your forms of music are bad, I am saying that the muse of astral entities is working through the bodies of many musicians at this time. When the light of lights descends to the form you call the physical realm, be

36

ready for the most amazing light and sound you have ever witnessed. Be ready and be aware, for the time is now that we speak of. Go in God's Love and work with your heart. Amen Selah and so be it.

Creation in Evolution

This information is channeled information by the guides Sananda and Sanat Kumara. The following includes questions asked by the Higher Self in order to help mankind understand what is going on in the physical plane.

What is going on with the energy surrounding the Planet today? So many people feel the clarion call and yet so many are not sure what is happening in their daily lives.

Sananda speaks:
The Planetary Logos, or the state you call a higher vibration of consciousness, is coming closer to the Earth Plane than ever before. What this means is this: the Christ Vibration is entering the physical plane at a much more rapid rate than ever before known to this Planet. As you know, no two objects can occupy the same space at the same time. This is a well-known fact of science. On a metaphysical level, no two energies can occupy the same force at the same time. Something will have to give. Either humanity will feel the

overwhelming force of the Christ consciousness and open up its heart, or the mind will try and force the energy away. If this is the case, then the Earth will have to go through a very painful initiation process. In other words, look at the Earth as a balloon. The spiritual energy is air that fills that balloon. If you blow too much air into the balloon, what happens? If you know what we are saying, then we feel we can now answer the second part of the question.

Sanat Kumara answers:
Before we answer your second question, I would like to add the following. Children of Earth, you have been given charge of a very beautiful Planet. You are truly the creation of the Highest of the High. Yet why do you try and separate one from another by looking at one as more evolved than another? You who say you are of the New Age and yet look down on those who you say "aren't as open as yourselves" are doing the same thing as others from other generations. You are witnessing the most amazing time that your part of the universe has seen in the history of your creation. Please pray for those less aware. Pray for your political and military leaders. On one level, what is also happening on your Planet is this.

The energy you call evil is an entity that has grown

over the centuries to become a power and a force unto itself. As you know, flus and colds are also entities. So let's keep this in perspective. Over the years mankind has focused mostly on the lower energies of self. Hatred, greed, envy, and lust for power have been the calling cards for this Planet.

Time after time we send messengers of light to make way for the Truth and Love. These are the only guiding forces in the Universal consciousness known as GOD. Man, having the capability to create with the power of the mind and affirming with the word, has set into motion one of the biggest struggles. All this is illusionary, we might add. You cannot see the Reality even though its energy is coming closer day by day.

As we were saying, through the years and after eons of verbalization, you have created your own monster. The energy your leaders are drawing from is the energy you envision them to have. If you think of them as evil or closed-minded, then by your own very power so shall they be. Oh, you workers of Light, this is no time to be weak of heart or of word or of thought. Do you not realize that by your very prayers and thoughts you can save your world!

This is the Truth. Open your minds to *Love*. Forgive on a daily basis. This does not mean to become like a group of cattle, afraid to speak your words. Just

41

be aware, those of you who say you know the truth, that right *now* your words are more power-filled than ever before. You are now tapping into the Christ Power. How can we understand this even further? How can we open up our minds and hearts and souls?

Sananda answers:
Dear one, do not look so wide-eyed at the Truth. Ye of little faith? Sound familiar? The Earth is moving from her third chakra or power position into her rightful energy of the heart. In doing so the power of man must be turned into strength. That is why there is a cry to go back to the way things were. Man instinctively knows that a big change is happening and almost all try and avoid it. He is trying to put all the pieces back into an old box. But he cannot do this. Man is moving forward whether he wants to or not. But man did ask for this change. Your relationship with God cannot go on like this any more.

As the Earth moves into the heart vibration, those of you on the path will feel a great deal of physical stress, and some of you may be noticing a shortness of breath as well as nausea and a pain in the heart. You are symbolically feeling what the Earth is going through. It is more important now than ever before to clean out your energy and ground yourself. We will explain how to do this as soon as possible.

If only ten percent of the Planetary consciousness would awaken to the clarion call of what is happening, the changes wouldn't have to be so great. On a physical level they say you only use one tenth of your mind's capability. If humanity would only get moving and open up ten percent of its heart capacity, this would be a beautiful change instead of a long-overdue baby being born.

Sanat Kumara speaks:
How can you open yourself up further? Very easily, my dear one. You start by waking yourself up to the fact that you are living with a child and that child is your own runaway thoughts. They are the destructive force on this Planet. That is right. It is your thoughts. We must attune ourselves to be the guardians of the gatehouse. The gatehouse is the opening to the eternal *Now* which all of humanity creates and sustains in this world.

Sanat Kumara continues:
The eternal *Now* is where the energy of *God* resides. Get in touch. Remain in the present, not jumping into the future of the Earth and worrying over the fact of whether or not you will be at the right place. Do not

worry if your loved ones will open up to be able to meet the transition. By your very thoughts you are creating and sustaining the worst that your thoughts have to offer. Of course, there are those of you who have no fear and are still generating plenty of thoughts of *Love,* but this is the reminder. We are trying to tell you in the simplest language we can how to change your very world.

In the past, those of the Mystery Schools knew the techniques and only passed them on to initiates of the highest order. Today we, or rather you, do not have this luxury. It has been eons of human development that have passed. You have taken only baby steps towards your own development.

How can you take control of this child you call the mind? Easy. By daily sitting yourself down in the morning and not necessarily meditating, (if you wish you may), but rather by verbally opening your mouth and supercharging the world, the substance, with your command. Say prayers of release and forgiveness. Open up your mind to receive the highest and best that God has to offer. Refuse to say ugly things about one another. Bless even the most seemingly ugly situations. Recognize yourself in others. Stop your elitist attitudes about your fellow man. You are all children of the Divine Creator. Not one of you is any more or any less special in the eyes of Divinity. Stop singling out your spiritual teachers and saying, "My teacher is better than yours," or "My channel is more highly developed than yours," or "My guides are clearer". Keep those childish thoughts to yourself. Many are here now doing the best work that they can. Granted, some may seem more clear than others, but that does not give you the right to be the judge. By your words, so shall ye be judged.

Sanat Kumara:
During the course of the day start blessing all around you. See the infinite glory known as God. Bless the Earth. Learn from your seemingly hard day. You created the lesson; now learn from it.

Sananda speaks:
Dear ones, the prayer I put out many years ago is still very powerful. Ye shall say it with power and strength. It is known as the Lord's Prayer. The words are about forgiveness and letting go.

What about forgiveness? What is the point of all this? Why say affirmations or pray out loud? What do our thoughts really project anyway?

Sananda speaks:
Forgiveness is what I originally was sent here to do. I spoke of turning the other cheek. This was to signify that Karma can only be a continuing lesson if we do not learn it in the first place. Then we must repeat and repeat. If we learn to observe our words and thoughts, we can control our actions, thereby creating an energy field which attracts to it the highest and the best in all that we do. The miracles that I did were only to show that to know the Law is to be the Master of the Law of Substance. Being a clear channel of *God,* we can use the energy that is all around us. Now, what does this have to do with forgiveness? I will tell you.

If we hold on to our negative experiences and sit down or walk around condemning ourselves or others for shortcomings or wonder why we haven't received this or that, you will notice the following. I will again tell a parable or a story. A young man always "seems" to be a day late and a dollar short in looking for his ideal job. In every relationship he is in it seems to go initially well; then it sours for him. He meditates and prays and even tithes to his spiritual organization. To the outside

46

world he smiles and talks of upliftment. Inside he is resentful and angry, not all the time, but enough of the time. He bargains with God for some miracle power to come into his life. Remember, he is an enlightened soul. He just can't seem to move ahead. Added to his condition are frequent colds and a financial situation that seems out of control. He goes to all types of readers and sends his friends and family the gold light of Love. Yet still he goes nowhere. This man is representative of the type of karma most seem to have. This man does hear the words releasing Karma but feels that he is not advanced enough to make it happen for himself. And ye shall know by your words, and by your thoughts shall ye be judged. Mankind hear me, once and for all. The crucifixion was for you. Transcend the bondage of hatred and fear of the unknown by forgiveness.

To make it even simpler: When you say words of forgiveness you wipe out or undo the Karma involved. Yes! Words and thoughts of forgiveness undo the yoke of bondage. That is the Divine Joke. You are the prisoner of your own words and deeds. And by their fruit ye shall know them. Forgive yourself first. Ask for forgiveness in all situations. The name of the Christ is very strong still. Ask and ye shall receive. I shall not enter your heart if it is filled with strangers. The strangers are the thoughts and words of bondage. Open up to make way for the highest to enter.

What we have to say is this, dear one. You must allow yourself to be open and forgiving more so now than ever before. We will not say what the future has to bring. We know that you are all developing separate realities right now on this matter. The only thing of importance is that you open yourself up to knowing the *God* is you.

You have heard this said over and over again. Many of you still feel that due to some personal limitation *God* will not welcome you into that next step. Please eliminate all thoughts of judgment to which you assign human characteristics. *God,* that consciousness, does not know judgment. This is not a new thought but one that must be brought up over and over again. You have given *God* human limitations, such as *God* is a he or she, or that this consciousness is happy or sad, or that you have some illusionary counterpart known as the *Devil.*

You must come to the understanding that you as a human being are in some way, shape and form limited to depend upon these narrow margins for some sort of shape and some identification. But let it be known that *God* just *is*. *Love* just *is*. You live in the *Now* and there is nothing we can do to explain the *plain truth*. You may try and understand by just noticing your breath now for a few seconds. As you do this, say over and over, "I am in the *now*". For a moment in time you will be experiencing reality, for in fact reality exists in eternity. To be close to understanding this is on the way to experiencing *God*.

We are bringing this through today so that you can stop being bewildered at the fact that some people use meditation as a guide to enlightenment and some use prayer. All these modalities are for the same pupose; it is to know *God*. Whether you give *God* the name of Buddha, Divine Love, or whatever, the basis is the same. You want to know that Mother Father Divine Creator. You feel as if you are an orphan and have a true need to know your heritage.

The Divine Plan

Sananda speaks:
On a daily basis we are throwing out energy. It matters not whether it is positive or negative, we throw out energy. If you feel tired at the end of the day, you have just "emptied out your being". Not literally, but you have given it up to every situation possible. You have spent yourself. What you are going to learn is how to get back all that energy you have given out. You take it back one hundred percent, purified by love. You will learn how to throw back to individuals anger that they give you and transform it into love. You will learn to transform your own energy, you will learn how to claim back your own space. You will learn how not to buy into other people's garbage. You will start taking full responsibility for yourself. You will also learn about your own chakras, because when you truly understand your own energy levels you will be able to understand how to heal yourself.

Sanat Kumara speaks:
The concept of Spiritual Masters. There is a growing

51

concern among us who work with the spiritual plane and with the Earth's plan of unfoldment. Never in the history of man have there been so many wolves around in sheep's clothing. Never before have there been so many people who work of things not of spirit but of things more of the occult and more towards, shall we say, working with power and magic.

We find it very sad indeed after centuries of warning. You have been warned not to be fooled, but to check the Master's credentials before you give yourself away body and soul. There has already been much talk about opiated saints. For those of you who do not understand, this is to put it out there to the readers. Find a Master yourself to follow to help you grow. You don't really follow a Master, you walk with a Master so that he can train you. If you want to learn to play tennis, you find a tennis master.

Humanity has got to understand the reason why everyone at this moment in time has such a feeling of anticipation. That anticipation is a letting go of old thoughts, a letting go of the old way, and allowing the person's personality self and ego to be released so that each and every individual on the planet Earth opens himself up to become a Divine Instrument.

Everything that is written about Prosperity is only 50% of the information that is truly available.

Everything that is written about channeling is only 35% of what channeling really is. What is known about healing is really very little. Regardless of what types of advancements humanity may think it has made on the spiritual path, it still has so much more to learn. It should really rejoice in that. Of course, there are individuals who have gone along the path and have worked and worked and worked. They have reincarnated and reincarnated and reincarnated. Where are they? Why, they are back on Earth, not necessarily by choice, but because they did not know how to implement the spiritual law on the physical planes.

Now there are a lot of fairy tales going on, stating that, "Those people *Saved* (and we say that tongue in cheek) are going to live on an ethereal, beautiful planet". There is even as we speak now a sphere denser than this one. Humanity does not remember from whence it came. There was a denser Earth; there was a denser plane of consciousness. This was at one time the "new Heaven and the new Earth" that so many people talked about. Refinement of this planet Earth and the refinement of this sphere of consciousness does not seem inevitable at this time. But what we do see are those individuals who can open themselves up to their own instrumentation to help bring about the heralding in of refinement of these Higher Spheres. This is why people must leave their bodies. It is not for punishment because they created such bad vibrations, nor that God has decided that He has to clean out the Planet every so often. It is because by Divine choice people decide whether they want to make the Earth Planes or this galaxy or galaxies that you see advance to a more refined state of consciousness. And there are those people who feel the fear of transcending into something higher. Believe us, it is not only just their ignorance.

There is a deep fear in many people who perceive themselves as rebels. They kind of relish the thought of thinking that they will meet a Devil. And we find it very sad, for what will meet them after their death is more of the angelic type of being who will have to calm them down and hold them and put them to rest. For when these people who think they are so demonic on the planet Earth do finally die and transcend to the lower astral planes, they will get to that plane of consciousness known as death. It is a lighter vibration than this Earth. They will be very disappointed to find that there is no punishment. The only punishment that they will have is that they will be forced to see their life played over and over and over again. Moment by moment, stopping the frames and replaying experiences they truly have to learn from and correct and adjust the next lifetime. And in that sense, that is where their hell comes from. Now those people by Divine choice have decided to go the way of the lower vibration Earth, which means there is a lower plane of consciousness where a type of humanity exists, hoping to evolve to this plane of consciousness which they think is a spiritual plane.

And then those of you who have finally gotten to this Earth plane level, you have the choice to advance to the next Earth plane level which you think is your spiritual level.

Are you getting the picture? You really never stop having a body. It is just a different type. In fact, our favorite joke song when people die, people who take themselves too seriously in a religious sense, is: "I ain't got no body."

This is information that has been lost. What seems to happen sometimes is this. Every single channel that brings forth information, depending on his or her limitation, depending on his or her willingness to open up as a full channel, will still limit the spiritual information that comes in out of the fear of being ridiculed. For even in channeling, sometimes they feel it is really better to go with the tide than stand with feet on the ground and say that you truly believe in God and aren't afraid to mention that word, and aren't afraid to mention the fact that the Christ conscious-ness, whose name is reborn in Sananda, exists.

For there are few who really tell the Truth, but everyone who channels tells the Truth according to their level.

Those beings, those like beings which are attracted to those people who deliver those forms of Truth, are showing you almost a physical representation of the spiritual planes of consciousness and what it is really like. There are some people who kind of get the point. Some people are tested along the way to getting the point. And then there are those people who just get it.

You are always drawn to the teacher and spiritual material you need for your development. Wisdom is knowing when to move on and release and let go, paving the way for an even higher *Truth* to come into your mind and heart.

The planetary alignment that is coming up is an alignment of the spiritual chakras of this solar system, the crown chakra being the Sun, Mercury and Venus being the sixth and the fifth chakras. The Earth on a heart chakra vibration is going out of the empathetic feeling of feeling everybody's pain into actually bringing in full force new life into this whole solar system. So that when the planets are in alignment, and those that walk within the light or within the Truth are meditating or just feeling the power of the planets, they likewise will be heralding in and lifting up the Earth as a celestial body. The solar system is a celestial body, helping to send out rays of consciousness to elevate those other planets where similar alignments are happening right now.

As is known, all of creation and all those people within creation come from Divine Mind. What we're about to explain concerning this spiritual growth period will be in the form of an analogy. Your solar system is guided by Sanat Kumara. In this sense the alignment of the planets with one another is elevating the spiritual mind of this Master. Even though Sanat Kumara is a Master, he will open his consciousness to learn more. The Christ operates and controls this Planet. The manifestation and transformation of the energies as Sanat Kumara increases and the Christ increases will raise up the energy levels of surrounding galaxies which will give Universal Mind a new thought, which will make Universal Mind possibly create a new Universe. That will be the only reason for the end of this one. It is not that you would stop existing as a person. You would be transformed into another energy with a different personality that would be raised into that finer vibration.

You may ask what you can do as individuals to raise your own consciousness. We say, "Be real". Stop justifying and patronizing and sublimating and affixing labels to yourself such as, "I am a vegetarian," or "I am this or I am that". Instead, you can say, "I enjoy being". Do you understand what we are saying here? Use that "I am" for what it is meant for, which is to bring in prosperity if you wish, or health. But learn to enjoy so you can "I am" in higher vibrations. When people start meditating, they may be stuck in the blues and the golds and the yellows and the whites. (The guides are mentioning the colors people focus in on while opening up different centers). We want people to start feeling their own vibrationary colours. There will be colors no one will be able to find on the Earth. That is how people can help herald in the newer vibration. Color, Light, and Sound are your image of who you are. The colors surrounding you are, in fact, the reason why you speak. Do you understand?

Spiritual Teacher is You

Concerning spiritual awareness: What are the steps, if any, to understanding what it is all about? There seem to be so many methods and so many teachers today. How do you decide?

Sanat Kumara answers:
Spiritual awareness is the total understanding of the soul. You have heard that God Realization is every person's birthright. This is true. You must first let that Divine Urge truly take you over. Have the courage to persevere. Many people become weak at heart over the journey. They feel, from stories they have read about someone else's initiation, that the path is too steep, too narrow, too involved, so that they don't continue on themselves. Many times they will blame some outside situation for refusing to go any further. Some people feel that they have become stuck and usually blame it on the lack of spiritual teachers in their area or whatever.

I feel that if you truly want to see spirituality first hand, as you have called it, you must be willing to give

59

up everything that you now call true. From the mundane perspective we are saying that you must give up worry, concern, doubt, fear, lust, greed, anger, limitation, manipulation, thoughts that generate separation on all levels.

So, you can see that the journey on the spiritual path is not for the faint or weak of heart. You will find that *responsibility for your words, deeds and actions* is what you are held accountable for. On the quest is a period in time known as the honeymoon period where you are so consumed with the information that you want to tell all of your friends. So be it. Silence actually works much better. But lessons need to be learned by all.

Then you will find that for awhile things may seemingly become harder than ever before. It is called sifting out what is true and what is false from your life. No amount of book reading can tell you what is false. Only you will know for sure what is true and what is not. Granted, there are universal truths that are changeless. Still, you have to decide for yourself what is truth and what is falsehood. Discrimination is very important on the spiritual path. Without it you become a tool or a puppet for those leaders that love control.

What we mean is that people learn to look to

channels or guides or teachers for their spiritual upliftment. This we say to you. Listen to what is being said. Do not be like the blind leading the blind. Learn to discriminate what is good for you, not for someone else. I don't care who the channel or the "teacher" is. Unless you feel the resonance of the truth within your very fabric, it is truth to the person giving the information, not you. Of course, things may ring true, yet you do not understand them. This is fine. This is called learning. Sooner or later when you hold on to a truth you will experience the meaning of it first hand and then and only then does it become truth in your heart. To just blindly say something is truth is no better than being a parrot that repeats what its trainer says, having no concept of what is being said.

Again, you cannot judge a person's level of truth. It is up to you as an individual to find your teacher or master. Whether it is the Christ, Buddha, Krishna or whoever, it is up to you to seek the highest and best that the Universe has to offer. If someone is following what you feel to be a false teacher, you have the right to hold that opinion, but never interfere with the growth of a student. To that person following this channel or that teacher or whatever course in spirituality they are following, it is the most important revelation they could be having right now.

And, of course, who left you in charge to judge the merits of that teacher? They are all here, large and small, to fulfill the purpose of teaching. Granted, we will talk of the opiated teacher, as well we should now.

There are those along the spiritual path that start feeling their charge and their power. What can happen is this. That is why we say the path is steep and narrow. You must never let your ego overwhelm you, to delude you into thinking that you and you alone are some great teacher of truth. This is truly the sign of someone whose ego is starting to take control. The danger to the person involved is a tremendous amount of Karmic debt that will have to be paid either this lifetime or the next. So, it is very important not to get so carried away by your limited amount of knowledge that you think, "Ah-ha, I have achieved it all. People are following XXXX. Do they not know of my great spiritual mind?" We will use the example of the opiated teacher in a story form.

There was once a young woman living in some town. She became aware of her spiritual capabilities quite by surprise. In the interim, she found she could channel a spiritual being. In the course of her opening, people started coming to her for readings. She, of course, at first was humble and still praised God for her capabilities. Then, over a period of time and some

years and readings later, she found herself with a
following of individuals that started giving her
feedback on her healing capability. Soon this young
woman forgot what it was all about and then her
"Guides" told her to start some community complete
with rules and regulations. She was the chosen one!

She was asked about other channels in a trance state
and she would seemingly always find fault with them
or their validity. She was starting to establish herself as
the Queen Bee.

Then she published a book by some Majestic Guide.
People from all over the country began to praise her.
And she totally accepted it. Then one day her
following became so large that when they would ask
her for blessings or miracles, they would appear.

What was happening was the people were
temporarily empowering her with their own energy,
creating for a time great capabilities for this soul. Still,
she forgot the true source of Divine Love.

She herself was starting to believe that only the
Magnificent Guide was the truth.

Time went on and she continued to gather
momentum and speed. Then one day she was called
upon for a great healing, and then, much to her
surprise, nothing happened. She blamed it on it not
being right or that the healing wasn't meant to be.

This continued to happen, and then her followers lost faith in her. What she was left with was a tremendous amount of Karma to deal with. Her lessons were now on power and strength and the misuse of spiritual law.

So, you can see you must always give praise to the one who created even the guides that come through you. Never interpret someone's spiritual gift of channeling as proof that the individual is a highly developed soul. Sometimes they are, but you must see the difference between the information and the person.

Anyone who claims to be a representative of God here to start some new religion or whatever . . . check it out in your heart and soul. Remember, we are in the time that Christ spoke about: "Many will come in my name, yet, I will know them not." Be aware that just because someone knows about Truth, it doesn't automatically make that person an expert.

You will choose your teacher by opening up yourself and hearing that teacher within first. Of course, it is helpful to have someone in the body who has made the journey before you. Learn to assimilate your own information and enjoy.

Secret Schools and Other Places

Sanat Kumara speaks:
Greetings on this fine day. We are here to tell you of the Universal Life Brotherhood. This has come to the name of those of the unmentionable. You have been taught to search out for that Brotherhood, and yet some of you are looking for it through people and different organizations.

This we say to you: The royal charge has been transferred to she who is the true high priestess of today. You look upon this as merely a formality, but this is what we say to you. Take the charge, all of you, as if you are truly candidates for that spiritual order. It does take discipline of thought and deed. Be still, you who follow the commandments of old, and open up to the channeling of the new. Follow and listen. The Lord of the Universe does speak through this channel as well as others. Do not become fooled by those who say there is only one way to God. The path is now narrowing. Those who cannot follow their hearts but only their minds will find themselves alone, and the gnashing of teeth that we have talked about

65

in the past will become a reality this day.

Let us tell you of the different schools now and for always. Open your hearts and not your mouths. Do not be so brazen as to think for one day or one second that just by knowing the schools you will automatically be a part of them. There are clarion calls to those who listen with their hearts and not their egos.

The schools will be explained. The White Brotherhood is also known as the School of Melchezadek. The Christ, Buddha, Salem, Moses, and others are a part of this school or order.

There is the Emerald Cross and the School of the Emerald Tablets. There is the School of the Essenes, which is also a part of the White Brotherhood. We are now going to tell you that there is a School in New Jersey as well as in Mt. Shasta, California and a few other places in the United States and the rest of the World.

We as a Planet are very connected to the Planet or Star known as Sirius. We have a school on that world that is working closely with the students and teachers in this world.

We have been watching the progress of your world for many centuries. We have sent space commands, so to speak, to come as your brothers to let you know you are not alone. We have come to world leaders in the past and they have not repeated or paid much attention to our pleas with them as a race. They have kept secret from you the intervention we have had with your scientists about nuclear war and destruction. We have come to them not in a dream but in the flesh. They still do not believe.

We, as your brothers in the spiritual sense and in the physical sense, we will be there as your Planet makes the great transformation. Some say the Earth will not go through the upheaval. We say, "Woe to you who do not prepare for the changes in the spiritual as well as in the physical".

We will appear as a squadron in the night talking to you on a telepathic wavelength. In order for you to travel with us, you must take on light bodies. This is accomplished by certain forms of meditation that change the molecular structure of your bodies. You must understand as well when we travel on space ships, as you call them, that means we are still in physical form. If we have transcended the physical, then we don't need space vehicles. Also know that all space beings aren't safe. Learn to discriminate.

Some planets are pure intellect. Here are the scientists that think nothing of gutting your animals for experiments.

Some planets are pure light, learning to balance the intellectual. This is supposedly the planet where you can balance the intellectual and the spiritual. Learn to balance, you people of Earth.

The planet Lucifer was a home to many of you before that planet blew itself up in the destruction of the ego. There is the asteroid belt between Mars and Jupiter. They, too, were where you are now. Dig deep into the memory of your race and learn to avoid what you have done many, many times before.

Sister of the Emerald Cross, you are welcome to come and ask any and all questions that need be answered by Lady Clarion and Monka. You are the blessed child that we have seen throughout the days of the last. Now what we have to say about our organization is very little. For you know the Emerald Tablets have to be released to only those of the initiated. The information can be given out. Still, only those with knowledge will be able to interpret them.

Step One is to be at peace with yourself and to truly see your lies and limitations. Stop justifying your existence and continuing to cause undue hardship to yourself and your fellow man. Learn to be in balance over your life. Learn to be the Master of your emotions. Your emotions are the dis-obedient children that run away from the Mother

Father Divine Creator of which you are a part. Learn to be what you are, not what people want you to be. Learn to listen to your inner voice. Learn that fun is a necessary part of life. To become rigid with our laws and to become a self-righteous being is to become a hypocrite in our eyes.

When you can give up all the trappings of this outer world existence that you call life, then you can truly live for Spirit. You must welcome death. It is the death of the ego that we are talking about. Know this and know this well. In death, all you know now is all you know now. It will feel extremely confining if you do not now become aware that the outside doings of man are, in truth, very insignificant to us. All that we see right now is a group of individuals becoming stronger in ego and power and not becoming stronger in the spiritual nature of things. You must become the example at all times. No matter who the individual is that is causing you some major upset, you must learn to use the discriminating power of the Christ and release and let go of that person. Otherwise, you will be held back in growth by your own slippery ego's insistence on slow growth and slow forgiveness. Remember, it is the ego that is fighting this battle on the physical plane. The illusion wants to take over this world. Somewhere along the line, the illusion has taken on a mind of its own and it thinks it is God.

God is eternal and never-changing. The outer world is always changing. The Truth is to be set free on the planet like never before, and it will rock the very foundation of every religion that is known to man today. Even the Mystical Orders are regrouping to take on the new orders that emerge. Go forth and speak the truth. Never before in the history of your Earth has so much information been available on a planetary level. We are here to give you the guidelines for change.

The organizations themselves are working with all workers of Light. Now is not the time to discriminate between who is clearer or who has more authority. *Only God* has the ultimate authority. For any woman or man who makes the statement that our words are not true, then it is the Death of the Lake of the Eternal Death for them. We don't say this with vengeance. This is what God has spoken in the past. Worry not, oh follower of Jehovah. The name of Sananda is truly a name with which mankind must become familiar.

The Emerald Tablets now come to life in the hearts of all mankind. Listen to the music within your soul. The musicians of today are truly inspired by all of the activating forces that want to release themselves before the cleansing of the planet. That is why there is so

much demonic music. The demons on the astral plane
want their message deeply instilled in the hearts of all
the children in hopes of loosing that energy into the
void, the void where all of this energy goes for a
millenium.

We say, "Be careful of the energy vibration that you
allow your being to be enfolded by." The energy will
work into your mind and into your soul. Listen to the
higher spirit of the Godself through different forms of
music. Allow yourself to see that you are guided. The
Emerald Tablets come alive today in the thoughts of
LOVE that you have for one another. It is no secret
that the Tablets have been inscribed into the hearts of
men, yet they open them not.

Do not blasphemously use the name of Christ to
wage war against those who are of different colors or
religions. Such fools these mortals be. The Emerald
Tablets are invincible and must be listened to or they
will crush out the bones of those with minds and hearts
of folly. Go in Truth.

Pay no attention to those who say that you are mad,
or, better yet, someone who is possessed by the Devil.
Oh fools of the Earth, ye ministers and false priests!
Yes, we dare to say false priests. You who believe in
the Devil and fire and brimstone, that shall be thy fate:
to work out in the astral the world that you have

sustained to the people in fear. The Lord of the Universe has no competitor. That consciousness that you try and give mortal consciousness to knows not the Devil, only varying degrees of love and truth. God just is and the Truth just is, and Love just is. The Devil is a poor excuse to blame on some other form for your mistakes along the path. Wake up to your own lies now before the morning comes again. We say to you that there is a handmaiden before you. She goes not out of her place to become like you who are all dressed in the clothes of the rooster. Be humble and yet exalt the God most high.

Have we not said you would be fed like the birds in the sky? Open your minds and hearts to receive the truth.

Do not think for one moment that a Master was always a saint. You must be all things before you can complete the path. Before meeting your guides that all of you are so interested in coming to contact with, you must make contact with yourself first. Listen to your own conscious mind to know yourself. You must be able to interpret what is right and wrong. You must be able to see clearly and take full responsibility for your own actions. Do not let spirituality become an excuse for laziness or let it become an excuse for fault-finding in others. Remember, this is not an elite club of individuals that are getting together to put the rest of the world down. Nor are you to take it upon yourself to try and save the world.

Cast not ye pearls before swine lest they trample them under your feet. This still holds true in the twentieth century. Be aware that if you are receiving information that you want to share with people, do so. Just understand that you must be able to deliver information that will not be falling upon deaf ears. Your inner quest will take you to a point of either supreme happiness or abject frustration. Remember that, more so now than ever before, it is important to keep in tune with yourself. And that phrase implies there is a celestial orchestra that hears your thought and plays the tune according to your thoughts and feelings. When you are true to yourself, that will be a harmonious setting. When you are listening to something that is no longer good for your development, you will feel the discord as things that will show up and stop you from going forwards. I want you to be able to hear that tune within yourself and learn to change the record or clean off the lint from your needle that is becoming filled with the dust or debris of some other pattern.

You must learn to ask for your conscious mind; then

you can work with your guides in a number of ways. Some of the ways and techniques you are already familiar with. Just ask that the Light within you reveal the Truth of the situation to you now. You must learn to trust and to be patient if your guides are to speak clearly and distinctly to you. Trust, do not manipulate, for the Law forbids hypocrisy on the path. If you dare to channel for someone else, please take note: we are no longer fooling and waiting for that long-distant appointed time. The karma will be instant if your ego is channeling and not the spirit of Love. Be aware of this note. And channels take note to clean out after channeling, if just for yourself. There will be many channels burning up and out of the Earth plane if they are not working with the energy properly. I will take care of my flock.

Sounds are Created from Light

First and foremost, the information that is coming through today is from Sananda. The thing we would like to make clear is speaking about Light. All of the Universe radiates on a Love vibration. Love, being a powerful energy, creates a sound. And the sound is AUM. Or the sound is I AM. As we said, Love is a powerful vibration; it is an energy. It is the Light. Light has sound. And to repeat, the sound is AUM. In like manner, every single individual has that individual Light or that individual life penetrating through it. You will know a man's enlightenment by the way he or she speaks. We have a tremendous amount of regard for individuals who do speak their mind.

But do remember it is better to allow yourself to digest what you are about to say first before you allow your words to pass through your lips. For, once your words have penetrated through the Universe, it is written down for all time. It is written down and it creates a vibration that either uplifts humanity or brings humanity down. This is why we say to people, and why the information is

75

so well known, that forgiveness is very important.

It is better for you to say nothing at all than to allow yourself to abuse that Power and that sacredness which words are supposed to be used for. Every word that comes out of your mouth is an activated prayer. This is not new information but this is information that needs to be heard again.

Now the reason we were talking about light and sound is that powerful Love vibration, which is entering into many people this day throughout the Universe, will be invoking that Universal celestial sound again. It is much easier for mankind to hear words first, than see light later. Man is working on his spiritual vibration and his lower self.

Scientists have come up with the Law that Light travels faster than sound because it is true. But on the physical plane it is the words that come first, creating the action and the energy. And man has to allow himself to become right in tune once again with that spiritual Enlightenment, or that Love which permeates the Universe. And allow that Love to guide his words as opposed to his words to guide his actions. This is very important for people to hear so that they may know as their thoughts go, so will their universe be created.

And this is why it has been said through various

channels that the more energy that is put upon the changes of the Earth in any way, shape, or fashion, that is what will happen. So be very careful at this time of what you formulate in the mind. Allow yourselves to rid yourselves of the thoughts that no longer apply to this new state of mind. So it is thoughts that should precede words instead of words, and then "Oh, I am sorry" later. But if man is still of that kind to speak first and think later, then he or she should allow himself or herself constant forgiveness.

While you are here on this planet Earth learning a succession of lessions and opening up your own spiritual development, you go through all experiences so you may learn about your highest good. It is only when you allow yourself the time to realize that hardship is an excellent opportunity to say "Yes, I must learn to rid myself of this condition that is holding me back from receiving my Divine Heritage."

But mankind takes quite a while before it realizes that these so-called punishments are self-inflicted conditions brought upon it for development and a good tool to learn forgiveness. Forgiveness is a releasing of the Karmic bind, which is the reason so many of you continue to make the same errors over and over again. Learn to forgive yourselves as well as other individuals that you feel are holding you back from your good. It is truly only you, anyway, that is holding you back. These thoughts act as a block that prevents you from seeing the Light. Have you ever tried seeing the day through windows that are filled with dirt and obstructions? It is almost impossible. It is the same way with inner enlightenment. How do you expect to see the Light if you have all these obstructions in the way? Learn to open up your heart and realize that God is a consciousness which is very close to you. GOD is YOU. Ask yourself to know yourself. Stop making up all these excuses why you must read more before you know how. Do you need a manual to know how to fall in love with a man or woman? It is called instinct. Open up the instinct of Divine Love and you will see that where there is Divine Love there is Divine Forgiveness. Do you hold grudges against anyone? Use this opportunity right now to empty your heart to the well of Divine Love to be in a state of forgiveness so that you may experience Divine Love. We are with you always. It is only when man awakens unto himself that he sees and says, "Yes, this is something I must rid myself of," but man being at the point of evolution that he is, we graciously allow him time to rid himself of those things which he feels are no longer useful in his life. For some people it takes a second; for some people it takes a few months.

The Heart Chakra – Love and Placement of the Earth

We will tell you what the statement of purpose is for this whole situation. The theme is a thread of advancing mankind and spiraling upward and expanding the consciousness and allowing people to know that the situation on the Earth today is a direct correlation with the attitudes that people have harbored deep within their hearts. The thing is not to eliminate the situation but to elevate humanity.

Some of the theories and some of the information that is being put out for the masses is not coming from clear sources. The fear and danger we find in this is that there seem to be a few elitist groups which believe that very few people, only those who feel that they are selected people, can channel through the *Truth*.

Many centuries ago, around the time of Buddha, prior to the Krishna, and even in times before the Christ, there seemed to be, off and on during the advent of spiritual upliftment, people who felt that they needed to corner the market on spirituality.

This is Lady Clarion, one who holds the keys to the Emerald Cross. Wake up, oh you small children of Earth! As has been said by Sananda and Sanat Kumara, the Earth will change. But do not go into fear. Rather go into yourself and try and help yourself to understand the great gift you have to open the Earth to her rightful place as the Heart center of this spiritual body you call a galaxy.

The Sun, as has been told, is the crown chakra and the earth is still exercising the consciousness of the third chakra. Enjoy yourself. See the Earth as she moves into the conscious level of taking over her rightful ownership. Then the spiritual council can meet with all of those who feel the strength within themselves. It takes courage, not a foolhardy approach to spiritual understanding.

No amount of meditation without the practical application on a daily basis of understanding the principles and the law will transform an individual into a spiritual Master. Please understand what I am saying. The message from this council based on the spiritual center known as Sirius is this: Learn to open your hearts. If you judge even your world leaders, then you are no better than those who asked for the condemnation of the unfortunate ones in war. We must learn to combat ignorance with Light, which clearly means that from the bottom of your heart you must empty out greed, lust and anger. You must become aware of the fact that the Christ consciousness is within you, waiting and ready to come out.

You can transform all of the above into *Love,* which means you are a strong warrior introducing into the world the concept of *Reality,* not duality, with its talks of evil and devils. This is one way humanity has for pretending it can't work toward Light.

In the first place, let us say this to you: We are here as Sanat Kumara and Sananda to communicate with you as if you were in front of us today. Be aware of the fact that even as we speak we are watching and guiding your footsteps.

High, high, high salutations, people of the physical planes. You are very aware of the fact that Christ will be coming to manifest fully on your Earth plane. His energy is gathering up force in all of you. Please be aware of this. The Earth as you know it is going to change so very much that many of you will leave your earthly bodies. Worry not over this too much. Some of you were meant to go to the next phase to reincarnate quickly on this plane as Light bodies. The transition of the physical and the spiritual will be too much for many to handle. As we have already announced to the Earth, the Spiritual and physical energy, when it meets

81

the amount of power and energy that will be unleashed, will be like nothing ever before remembered in the history of human evolution.

Worry not over the fact that the Universe is going to change. For it is not just the Earth, but as the Earth as a spiritual body of consciousness helps evolve the spiritual being known to you as a solar system, then mankind as cells of the Divine Mind will truly create a celestial body and finally realize that which has been waiting to be realized since the formation of this galaxy began. The truth of the situation is this – the Universe as you know it is, for lack of a better explanation, the formation of Divine Mind in an effort to know itself better. And to keep itself company, it created all forms you now see and many things that your finite mind would have a very difficult time understanding. So, in an effort to know itself as Divine Love, images and replicas of thoughts and all dreams were created.

All that you see is known as the world of illusion. When consciousness such as yours tries to totally unbalance the world of duality, then an intervening force known as the Spiritual Council steps in to help those that are not adhering, for lack of a better terminology, to the boundaries which mankind can move. Your whole purpose is to be a total expression of LOVE. That Love is for the creator who sustains and supports you by remaining in a state of Bliss and Sleep, for lack of a better description.

Think of it this way: You are asleep and you are coming to realize something, and then a group of undesirable actions come into that part of your consciousness. You either wake up or change the dream. Well, in epochs before, the dream was changed, i.e., the earth changes of Atlantis and Lemuria. It seems as if you have been given the opportunity, with the help of Divine Messengers, to enhance that sleeping state into a state of divine reality, but the effects of the drug of sleep or coma keep humanity chained into believing that you are indeed the ones who can keep the universe moving. Wrong. That is not the way it is. Take heed, oh you small children. As we have said before, the coming of the energy will be for those who have tried as best they can to undersand the fulfillment of the law and welcome the awake state of God which will mean, in short, the annihilation of the Universe. And when that consciousness puts the energy back, those of you who work in harmony will be made manifest as beings of Light enjoying the next evolutionary plane of consciousness. There is a planetary council known by some, and then very few actually will accept the fact that the Earth is the last planet in this gross plane of consciousness to accept the law.

You have this to think about: If you only use ten per cent of your mind on the physical plane, just realize that less than ten per cent of you are even interested in the spiritual mind. What a difference you could make in the change that is to come! Do not hold yourselves back. Enjoy your *Love* and learn to release and put into perspective *now* what is important. So be it and Selah.

You must become modern man, not the children who were created eons ago. Those of you who have evolved have used only your intellect with which to handle your affairs. Your emotional bodies are very underdeveloped. You have the capacity for change. As was said, you who do not heed the call will be indeed made manifest to a plane of consciousness which is lower than this one, so you may try and evolve again. We have communicated to those in government and they have not heard our Plea. We have spoken to messengers in the past, and you have not heard our Plea. We are speaking to you now, and within ten minutes some of you will become angry over something that is nonexistent. The time to try to implement the *Law* is now. You have a very short time in which to change your ways. This is not a threat but rather a direct communication. The Earth as a conscious being is going through labor pains as she gives birth to a new consciousness. Won't you celebrate with her and become the proud inhabitants of a new growth period in your spiritual development? Enjoy yourselves always and know that Divine Mind is here to answer any and all questions. Preach not words which will frighten, for the time for courage is more important than fear. The parent within you should nurture your children known as the Mind.

Power and Freedom

When Jesus Christ was out in the desert, he was coming into his own power. At that moment, something happened as a reminder to us all. He was offered wealth and total dominion over the people of earth if he would give power to the Devil or, as the Native Americans say, his darkside.

Christ went through a lot of changes out in the desert searching out who he was: a Deliverer of Truth. He could quite easily have given in to that dark side of himself (Yes, *himself*) and walked away with ultimate control over all. But that is not what he saw fit overall. He was very aware of the darkside and spent much time with the masses exchanging information about how to protect themselves from it.

So, what is the meaning of power in the real sense of the word? To some, it may mean control over someone emotionally or the need to force others to follow their belief systems. Power means different things to different people. Just as some like to control, others give their power away in relationships.

On a certain level, there are belief systems, religions, parental training and other forms of conditioning that can make it almost impossible to change unless you start to look carefully and then recognize that maybe you have surrendered your power.

One of the biggest changes you can make in reinstating your own power is to realize that all it takes is to believe that you can do so. Power is the capability of creating your own reality and believing in yourself one hundred per cent – not the small you, but the you that is totally connected to God.

When one person tries to control another, what usually happens is that the same energy and intensity of restriction usually backfire and become the person's own undoing. You can never control or own another. This is a Universal Law.

That is why when you really release and let go of someone and allow God and Love in its place, then balance will truly follow. That is trusting in the God power. With the same power, you can create such tremendous change in your life that no one will recognize you.

In order to achieve power one must understand that no word, deed or action goes unnoticed in the Universe. The sum total of your life today is by your own very nature and what you believe in. Whether you are poverty stricken in consciousness or wealthy in spirit is totally up to you. Whether you are in a great relationship or one of a truly foul nature is how you think about what you deserve as a companion or what you are willing to put up with. Your career is either your true calling or what everyone expected you should become or what you thought you could have. Your health is how you feel about all things in nature. And so on and so on and so on.

You do not have to be a spiritually evolved master to get a grip on your own life and steer your own destiny. The path that you will follow is not one for the faint hearted. It will require you to really make some strong changes in your life, but, if you follow them, you will see the rewards and will be on the road to happiness and self fulfillment.

In order to create change you have to learn to let go of some things: things that are worn out and outdated, things that strangely enough have been the very albatrosses you wear around your neck and complain to the world about.

Freedom: that is a frightening word to some people. They think it means loneliness. In reality it means to be in alignment with your true self and work out things in the NOW and to be at one with the Divine Plan that you were originally brought here to fulfill.

89

You see, when you start eliminating things that hold you back from your true self you start becoming free. People, usually parents and friends, at first will start telling you you are giving up years of security, but usually what they are doing is just reacting because all of a sudden you are not asking for or following their advice any more or feeling sorry for yourself and feeling guilty. When you start really changing, you start feeling your connection to God in the greatest sense of the word.

So how to start on this lifetime journey into the unknown? You first look at your life and what you would change if you could and know that you can. You don't always have to end relationships or careers or anything that you are already altering yourself. All that follows will be a natural undoing of the unnatural that is in your way of God. God is the primary focus and the goal is to follow the laws of God and integrate them into everyday life, to become more joy filled in your approach, to truly have balance in all areas of your life and to be the Creator of your own Universe. You and all things that the eye can see have been created by God; all the mysteries that you can think of in the metaphysical sense are Laws that govern the Universe.

Words, especially, can cause us to become off

center. Just think of some statement someone may have made to you and feel how off centre you can become. Everyone, no matter who they are, is affected by the power of the spoken word. Just think of some words you may have had with a loved one and the feelings of despair that sometimes can follow. Then an explanation or maybe an apology can smooth the whole thing out.

You also have to be aware that words thrown into the wind can never be taken back. Once something has been said, it is as good as manifested. People wonder why fate has been unkind to them when they pray so much to God. Often it is because on one hand they are blessing and praising God but, more often than not, they are condemning the world for all things. That is not to say that a casual remark has no power. All words have power, and who controls those words? Why you do! When they said the word was made Flesh in the Bible, they weren't just talking about the Christ, they were also talking about the Christ Power you have in claiming your own highest good.

Emotions

Sananda and Sanat Kumara speak on emotions and how to work with them properly.

Sananda speaks:

I have come today to speak on working with your emotions. There is no doubt that, in the realm of life, this issue must be addressed. People have for years been trying to figure out what emotions are. Some people think that it is a conditioned response that needs to be looked at with a psychological eye, while others feel that it is a hindrance on the way to spiritual growth.

This is what emotions are. They are acute feelings of the Universal urge to know itself in a limited form. You may look at it this way as well. When you are thirsting for something in an intellectual realm, the mind naturally gravitates towards a book or a series of lectures to satisfy the urge to know. When you are in school and the professor or teacher says you are to have a test on information that you should know inside and out, there are many responses that one would have: one of relief so that you won't have to carry the

93

information in your head for much longer; or a feeling of sheer panic because the information didn't sink in; or a feeling of desperation because you didn't take the time to study.

In this final example you can see why emotions are important for your spiritual growth. The aspirant on the path is like the student with the teacher. The teacher is God within, trying to express itself through a limited form, in order to simplify the way the knowledge comes in the lessons in the school of life. The emotions are the story that is being told in the lessons. If you can understand your feelings and work with them properly, then you can really get to see the overall plan that is being laid out in your study of life. So you can eventually graduate through the schooling and get busy in the real world to do some work.

Like the student, many of you stay stuck in some lesson in the path of emotions. Taking the path of least resistance isn't always the way to go. For all the emotional charge that you may be avoiding is being stored up in a universal capacitor sometimes known as karma and will release itself for the charge has come to overflowing. This is why people feel burned out after working out a bad experience. The overflow of energy that is being discharged many times is too overwhelming for the instrument or being it is being conducted through. The clearer the person is in handling the emotions on a daily basis, the easier the discharge will be for that individual.

To understand electronics or any of the sciences is to understand in part human nature. A part of our lesson is a basic lesson in electronics. Your mind and spirit are like circuits. When you are building an understanding and wanting to know about life, you are opening up the circuit to allow a greater charge to come through – meaning you are now willing to take charge of your life. But when you resist the lessons, then you in essence have cut out the life force that is truly the God force from entering your life. When you do this, then the circuitry breaks down.

This is where emotional as well as physical problems come in. You are not handling your energy, charge, or in other words, emotions, properly.

Now we are not saying that you must go into denial or a hard time. This is not what I am saying. If you are in a rough period right now, you must look at the overall events and see how you have been handling your situations in life all along. Do you prefer for someone else to tell you what to do? Do you say, "Oh well, I guess it was meant to be"? Or do you look it squarely in the eye and try to force a change? Or do you look at what is going on, feel the emotions, let the emotions happen, then look at how you react in similar situations so you can move to the next lesson? Or do you do all of the above? It matters not to us how you handle the situation. What you must do is handle it properly. What we feel is proper is to let go of all guilt connected to anything that you do. Look to the Source for forgiveness. Look at your lesson and be ready to take on the full responsibility that goes along with acknowledging what is truly going on. If you are at fault, then acknowledge that. If someone else is responsible for the situation, then don't gloat over someone's situation. You must learn the key word. It is responsibility.

Creating Your Own World

There is a lot of talk about the New Age and that the energy is coming through a lot quicker. Exactly what does that mean to the everyday person? What is the feeling of expectancy, and how are the karmic connections that we are making as a whole being worked out if this is supposedly the end of this cycle?

Sananda speaks:
That has been explained by many, but we will explain that again. The coming New Age which you are already in is the heralding in of the forces of the Light. What that exactly means is this. People are beginning to grow at a rapid rate of development. You no longer have to worry about waiting to reap your rewards, so to speak. Whatever you do as a person will come back on you a lot quicker. There is no time like the present to get yourself in tune with what your motives and what your true desire and intent are all about.

People who embark on this life path especially now will see that their Karma, or the way that they balance the way they deal with people, will come back to them

97

right away. Like your famous person Newton said, for every action there is an equal and opposite reaction. This is the law of Karma in a nutshell, to use your vernacular. Whatever you think, so shall it come to pass. Judge someone and so shall ye be judged. Think good words and good deeds, and so it shall come to pass the same for you.

People in this age have to realize that the stuff that God is made of is more available today, so to speak, than ever before. Yet, you wonder why the balance of the world is off. Just give yourself one moment to think who created this condition. The people in it. The Race Thought of today must be purified. The acting *Evil* of today is really the manifestation of years and years of conditioned thinking of the ones called mankind.

You have free will to create whatever kind of world you want. What you see is what you have asked for. When people say it is a cruel God that created this, man is now giving *God* humanlike characteristics. *God* is *Love*. Man has free will to create whatever he or she pleases.

Due to the effective workings of the mind, if people would get together and eliminate from the mind fear, separation and lack, they would see that this New Age or the feeling of expectancy truly is about mankind becoming Sons of God, not just in the sense of some elitist group of individuals that call themselves the enlightened ones. They would see that all of mankind has that option at this very moment in time.

Can you not see that the time is now?

Look at it this way, if you still can't quite grasp the Truth of the situation. Many people are now prophesying, and many of them are saying that the way to the Truth is through them, or their guide is one of the chosen this or that. On some level the Truth wants to come out. Some people are using this as an opportunity to make a great deal of money, and some are using it to satisfy the ego. Whatever the intention, when that dynamic force of spiritual Light breaks through on the Earth plane, the Truth will be so strong that you will not be able to misinterpret the way the Truth feels.

That is the expectancy that everyone is starting to feel. You have to admit that the Earth cannot go on the way it is now; something has to give. That is why many people are concerned about doom and gloom. That is what everyone has been programmed to expect. It is like the child that is so bad all the time that it just knows that the parent is going to reprimand him for some crime of being a child.

Let go of that fear. Mankind, hear us out! It is the

time to step into the NOW and to start to create the world that is and has been waiting to emerge. You have everything in this world to establish life and sustain it indefinitely.

Learn to sustain life where it first starts, in the mind. Connect and re-align yourself with the one called *God*. You also asked about the end of this cycle.

Why is it that I am misquoted on this statement? You must see that a cycle is a period in time that it takes mankind to grow in awareness. Never since the time before Atlantis sank have so many come out of the closets of spirituality. Closet psychics. The cycle's end celebrates mankind's coming of age. This is important to understand. At this point in time, many of you are at the age of two or three. What does a two- or three-year-old do? Just observe. MINE. MINE. MINE. EGO. EGO. EGO. My toys are better than yours. And when told by a parent to do something, the child says NO.

It is likewise with the people of Earth today, whining and crying about the state of world conditions, equality, spiritual freedom, poverty, wealth, politics, relationships, possessions, and even about spiritual belief systems. The cry is the same in most places. My country is better than yours, my family is better than yours, my concepts of God are more new age than yours, etc., etc. World leaders act like children with rather large, colorful rattles. They hold up their nuclear weapons and ideologies as if they were some kind of symbol of spiritual freedom. Children playing adults. You must all become examples to one another and stop this foolish and dangerous game of acting like two-year-olds. Grow up before it is too late to change. Start now with yourself and see yourself blessing your world leaders so that the Light of Christ enters into their hearts. Bless all situations so that they can be released. Release from the mind poverty and separation of the races and belief systems. Work in a vibration of Love to eradicate the limitation that is crowding in the world today.

Expectancy? I would say that it is the sole desire of everyone alive today to see balance. After centuries of fighting you must see that fighting hasn't solved anything. It is the EGO saying, "Look at me and how different I truly am."

What is the EGO and how does one control it? If you are saying that it is too late, does it mean that no matter what we do at this point the Earth is doomed? Then what happens to free will?

101

Sanat Kumara speaks:
The ego. The ego is a part of the universal life stuff that is called Self. The Self is broken down into many individualized parts. There is the part that is God self. There is the part that is spiritual essence in the etheric body. That is the part that is connected to the God self or the higher self. Then there is the personality, which contributes to some people's demise and is called the ego. What is this thing and why get rid of it? The ego is on a search-and-destroy mission, so to speak. The ego is a part of this stuff called into the world of illusions, the very same world most of you are in right now. You can only see the outside trappings of what the outer world seemingly portrays as reality, and you become trapped in it. This is where the ego thrives. When the ego is at its height, it wants to relish its separateness. That is why people are sad, happy, world famous, unknown, spiritual, unspiritual, etc., etc. Any way the ego can, it will try to separate itself from the whole of existence and see itself as separate and special.

The ego knows intuitively that as soon as a person becomes involved in spirituality the ego is on the way out.

That is why it seems to be so hard to get started on the spiritual path. The ego is going to die. Along with the death of the ego goes the death of the world of illusion, which means you still retain your individuality, but are immersed, seeing everything as God and God in everything. Your personality self no longer exists. You transcend death. Even death is the world of illusions. The ego perpetuates the play of agonizing experiences and experiences of pleasure to prove that the game must still go on.

So what does the ego do on your way along the spiritual path? It says that "I am Good" or "I am Bad". The ego seems to find great pleasure in singling itself out as spiritual. So you can see that the ego is like a bar of soap or liquid mercury, very hard to hold.

The ego in a wild sort of way is the God of the world of illusions. People pray to it. Famous stars are idols. Money is worshipped like the golden calf was many centuries ago. People clamor to be different, not accepting themselves for what they are, but rather for what they are not.

The ego even disguises itself as good intentions. How many people examine their hearts for what they are doing? The ego gets great pleasure out of being told what a good person it is. So much for a limited description of the ego. How does one control it? By letting go. Letting go of the feeling of separateness or that others have control over you. See yourself working and walking on a path that is geared towards God.

The ego can be given up to that belief in the overself or by staying in tune with the higher self. The ego cries for separateness. The voice of release is a joy-filled experience. The ego will give you one million reasons why you are not prepared or good enough for this experience. The higher self welcomes you the way that you are. The ego will say that you are too old or too involved with your current lifestyle to give up what you are. The God within knows that you gain everything and give up nothing. The ego will say it is a lonely life to release the ego. The God within knows that you are truly coming *home.* The ego says, "I have heard it all before and still there is no difference to my life." The higher self will say nothing and just patiently wait. The ego will think that it takes lifetimes. The higher self is always with you. So, you see, it does take some conditional commitment from you to want to be able to stop blaming the world for your ego-related problems and admit that you are in the situation you are in because you want to be. You just have to release and let go. It is that simple. Take it one day at a time, one step at a time. Realize that you don't just pop out of bed and run the Olympics just because you feel like it. It does take some sort of training to get yourself disciplined enough to be able to make the journey.

A regime of good deeds and good thoughts on a

daily basis for about 15 minutes a day would get you started. A healthy attitude about your life and the world you live in will also be a diet that we can recommend. See your faults and do not dwell upon them, but rather take the bull by the horns and start to shake off the centuries of programming and let yourself know that you can overcome any personality flaw because the truth is that you are a part of God and God is perfection. Start seeking the teacher within yourself for the answers to your questions. Start reacquainting yourself with the Higher Self. When someone annoys you, do some quick research to find out if he is just mirroring what you don't like about yourself, and then let it go. I am not saying lose your capability of discrimination, nor am I saying become an irresponsible person under the guise of New Age axioms. Rather, take stock of yourself and become truly responsible for who you are and the condition of your world. If your life is all mucked up, so to speak, and you say you are on the spiritual path, then look closely at what you expect to have happen in your life. Release and let go. Now that should be perfectly clear.

Of course you have free will. That is why we have told you to watch your progress. It is not too late in the ordinary sense of the word. What we mean is that your free will is dictating how the Earth will respond to the incoming energies. You dictate how the energy will respond on the Earth.

Daily Living and Expectations

*To understand patience and how to apply it in our daily lives.
How to release and let go of all unwanted emotions that seem
to overload us on a daily baisis.*

Sananda speaks:
First understand that patience is an emotion, so to
speak. It is an attitude, and to be able to understand
how to apply it you must first experience it.

All people in their daily lives have mothers or fathers
or brothers or sisters or someone that they just can't
seem to strike that balance with. This does not make
you a bad person. This means that these individuals do
not truly· allow you to take charge or you do not let
them take charge of their own lives.

Somewhere in the recesses of your mind you have
allowed this person at some point in the relationship to
take charge and you have never reclaimed the energy
back to its proper owner, YOU. So what seemingly
happens is that you become uneasy and impatient
because there is a desire to reclaim that energy or
power. Or you want to give up that energy or power.

When you can see that no one person on the Earth today has any claim or right to take your own feeling of personal power, then you will be able to exercise patience in almost any situation. You need to empower others as well, meaning to give back to individuals what is truly theirs. People unknowingly give other people in their lives an unrealistic view or opinion. And when that person does not meet up to your expectations, what sets in is impatience with that individual and how he or she has let you down.

You see, that person did not let you down. No one can. You let yourself down by having false expectations of that individual. Impatience is a form of anger. It is a subtle form that creates the same amount of turmoil in the physical body and creates stress as well as creating a chemical imbalance. That chemical imbalance can lead to creating negative energies in the body. With enough imbalance disease can set in.

Just take the time you need to really examine any situation that you are in and really look over your motives for sending such energy out of your system.

To look at yourself and to be able to identify the situation is the first step along the way. Don't continue to bury your head under the sand and say, "Oh well, I just made another mistake." You end up with that continuous cycle of making yourself feel guilty. And as you may know, guilt is a luxury emotion that justifies feeling bad over what we did so we can continue to punish ourselves to prove we really are sorry. Then in comes worry, and now we go full cycle because you become impatient with yourself for not handling the emotional situation the first time.

All of this stems from the ego making a valiant effort to prove how separate we are from *God*. Now, how do you identify these emotions and put them to rest? First, you must start to realize that you are programmed since childhood in terms of how to act in the world. This is another subject that we will cover at some other time.

You must learn to come out from under the covers and stop blaming your parents or yourself for your cruel or, at best, so-called unspiritual behaviour. Put it to rest on that matter. You are going to learn how to take the bull by the horns and create your own life.

People go through lifetime after lifetime being someone else or working out how to truly be themselves. In the course of a lifetime you may get stuck in an emotional rut. You react the same way to certain situations. That is how people look at one another. For example, "Oh, don't get too close or joke with Bill too much; he really has a bad temper." We program ourselves and let other people see our program by how we display our emotions. Or, "That Sally really always is in such a good mood."

Now, we are not inferring that men are always angry or women are always happy. That is not the point. What we are trying to say is this . . .

You, as always, have the option to accept your situation as it is and then look, reflect, and allow yourself to enjoy it or learn to change it.

110

Relationships

What is the importance of relationships? How do we attract our correct partners? What about the issue of sex?

Sananda speaks:
The coming new age poses problems to some of you in regard to relationships. You are expecting some person who will come into your life without any problems whatsoever. A true partner comes to you by reflecting your images of what a relationship should be.

So, in other words, the person you choose is the person you have dreamed up in your mind. It is what you are expecting out of a relationship. So, if you are in the wrong relationship it is because you have finally awakened to your needs. Many times people will go through many "bad" relationships because they do not really believe they deserve a good relationship. They may have the right understanding of *God* in a spiritual sense. But they limit the good of *God* to the things that they think *God* should be involved with. You must understand that the reflection of yourself will be seen in your partner. If there is growth, then accept what your lesson is.

Now let's address those of you who are single. If you really want to be with a partner, don't put such tremendous limitations on that person that you are trying to attract. In order to really open yourself up to the right relationship, you must be able to clearly see in your mind's eye the type of energy you want to surround yourself with. Be specific with the type of qualities you want, but don't limit yourself to this and only this. How do you expect Divine Love to be activated if on the one hand you trust *God*, but on the other hand are so rigid in terms of what you will be able to let in your life? Ask for the perfect partner selected by *God*.

Relationships don't mean scheming or crying or waiting or pain. Nor do they mean the end all and be all of creation. Don't think that you are exempt from life if you are by yourself.

Relationships in the purest sense mean being able to see yourself in one another, learning to let go of labels, being compassionate and understanding. Relationships help you to truly learn the law of forgiveness and to be able to see the daily activating force of Christ consciousness in one another.

Relationships help you to not just tolerate but to accept, not want more out of a person but to communicate needs. Do not stay in a lust vibration but transcend and learn – about true passion and strength and selfless sacrifice. So, in order to see why you haven't allowed the balance to occur, look within and see if you are working on outdated thinking concerning what relationships are. Are they truly your images or are they what someone or something gave you?

Remember, take the time alone to really sort out what you want in your life. It does take some bravery to walk out of some old situations. Ask for the help of God to be there in making all the right decisions. The Divine Love will never steer you wrong. Now we are not saying that all people are in the "wrong" relationships. For your relationship is always correct according to the situation you are in. Remember, we create our own realities. What I am saying is that if you feel that it is outdated, then it is time to change it or move on.

In order to simplify this, let us just say this: Mary has been in a relationship with a man for three years. For two out of the three it has been torture that she has to put up with. Praying for a change in Joe, he never seems to change, yet she is unwilling to think that there could be a mismatched energy. So, it continues on. Meanwhile, Mary is surrounded by many people who say, "Leave him." She gets angry and stays on to prove that it can get better. Meanwhile, she is praying for her perfect partner. Now, a young man shows up in her life who really gets her attention. But this young man also has a girlfriend. "Nevermind," thinks Mary, "this will make the change." So, out goes Joe from her life. Now she asks Bruce to stay. He can't, he says, because of his girlfriend. Mary is shattered. Has God pulled a practical joke on her? No, it is just that like attracts like. Bruce wanted to know if he was still in love with his girlfriend, and Mary just happened to come along.

Mary was still looking at relationships as hard to come by. She still felt that relationships were not consistent or reliable. She created the same situation with another person, complete with her partner having another partner, just like herself. So, days of sorrow and self-exploration occurred until one day Mary looks at what she truly wants and lets God handle that situation for her. Soul-searching shows her that trying to force love or any situation will not cause right results. Let go and let God.

So even in marriage, if the situation seemingly looks unbearable, know that on some level you allowed this to happen because of your great imaging power. Don't

✠

let Christ within you sleep. Awaken the highest
healing power of the Christ within and call upon that
energy for a healing and a restoration.

Also remember when there is continual conflict and
stagnation that these are the moments of the greatest
healing. Look at the lessons involved, bless them and
release them to the highest of the high. The mistake
some people make is to take the whole burden upon
themselves and not let go and let God or their higher
self work out the situation for them. We are not saying
life will be one rose after the other, but at least you will
let your Divine Plan unfold and not stay closed up.
Open yourself top to bottom and rejoice.

So you want a loving relationship. First establish
one with yourself and realize you must be able to like
yourself. Establish what you truly want out of life.
In giving up all to God your life has more of an
even flow. When you adamantly force thoughts like
my partner must be hot, must be Italian, must be rich,
etc. and so on, you are limiting yourself to what the
universe has in store. So it comes from a point of
feeling you won't be attractive to your correct partner.
It's one thing to affirm, pray and visualize for your
partner and it's another thing to look at established
ways of dealing with partners. Maybe you have
inadvertently been seeking the highest but "putting up

with" not the highest because quite honestly that is all
you believe you deserve. In writing down the way
relationships are for you in the present moment, how
do you respond to issues? Do you try to manipulate
relationships by planning your every move? "Well, if I
say this or do that I will get this type of response." Or
through fear, not make your feeling or demands met
even though change is necessary. Do you berate
yourself, wonder why you don't receive flowers,
compliments, think arguing and fighting is important
but painful, feel that you want your partner as your
friend but think, oh no, it can't really be?

What is your idea of a relationship – healthy, loving,
confining, restrictive or what? What are your feelings
about enjoying a good life with all people supporting
you? Too good to be true? Why do you want so much
yet expect so little?

You in every phase of your life have the capacity to
receive LOVE from God.

Sometimes situations in relationships take time to
mature – to be open and *communicate* is more important
than sex, possessions or anything. The more open the
communication the more room there is for growth
from both parties. But what if they won't hear me?
Why can't they listen? Learn to improve your
dialogue. Try new ways of approaching each other.

Learn to speak from the heart. Try replacing "you hurt my feelings" or "I'd die without you" etc. with "When you say this – this is how I feel" or "I am interpreting you to mean – is this true?"

Then put down the boxing gloves and listen openly. Yes, sometimes there is a sting in Truth and differences of opinions are healthy.

If you can come together in LOVE to share and communicate, God's presence will always be in the relationship. Remember, when Christ said if two or more of you gather in my name my presence will be there. And in the sanctity of two souls meeting and forming a bond of LOVE, the Christ force is ever present. Willingness allows the relationship to attain to new heights. People believe that believing in God means a dry relationship. This could not be further from the Truth. The Fire of Love rekindles Passion on all levels – passion for living and loving is important. In true partnership you can collectively work out tremendous amounts of karma together. You can be there for one another and at the same time be exclusive and separate. Love stops selfishness and teaches you selflessness. Sacrifice from a holy view and a sacred understanding of the briefness of life.

All too infrequently do couples take each other for granted and allow Love to die. If one only knew the day of your appointed Death, life might have more meaning. But pettiness and childishness is the cause usually of the breakup of all couples. Where real love is established, *no one* can break that bond.

If you can see the God in one another, then truly you have found Love. Again, feelings of jealousy or possessiveness must be met and worked out. Remember, you are working to create balance and harmony, not to create bondage. God's Love alone can bring couples together. It is the God in you that recognizes the God in your partner.

In metaphysics – *like attracts like*. So look deep and see what you put out in the Universe. Listen to your words, deeds and actions and what you believe you deserve will come to you. Never limit your good; let go and let God handle the situation. Let the Christ in you reflect and nothing but your highest and best partner can come to you. See it happening *now*.

Affirmation

Words are incredibly powerful.
Words bind and create a reality.
Your thoughts put those words into action.

What you say and believe must be in harmony for all things to come to pass and herein lies the Truth.

God has promised every single thing that is created: shelter, love and food and companionship and perfect health. It is only when we allow ourselves separation from our Divine Parent and we refuse to see our divine heritage that our supply is cut off.

We must have faith and unswerving belief that God will provide for us.

We cannot expect to see this world in lack and then wonder where our supply went, or see love affairs as painful then wonder where is my partner.

When people have full faith, courage is not far behind. Sometimes it is in the eleventh hour that those miracles do appear.

Affirmations are words of power that should not be taken lightly. Every word out of your mouth is a

✠

prayer and should be treated accordingly. With your words you can create or destroy, manifest or block, bring peace or war – love or hate.

Working with I AM calls in the God force. So always be aware of what you say with the I AM. Always be aware of these things.

Through words, Christ raised the dead, healed the sick and fed the multitudes, and you can acquire things or change conditions in your realm just by believing it and speaking it so.

It takes practice to let go but more practice on letting things come to you. Just open up and write down every pain or problem, any things said and done to create harm to you or things you may have done to others. Then, one by one, release them by verbalizing out loud: "I am releasing this to the forgiving Power of God; all these things are now dissolved and forgiven." Everyday release a little more – then you know it's released when it doesn't hurt you anymore or you no longer feel the sting.

Then spend time affirming out loud:

I AM – LOVE

I AM – BLESSED

I AM DIVINELY FORGIVEN

I AM PERFECT HEALTH

I AM DIVINE ORDER

I AM BLESSING EVERYONE AND EVERYTHING IN MY LIFE

I AM OPEN TO GOD

I AM LETTING THE CHRIST IN ME REVEAL TRUTH

I AM TRUTH

I AM IN MY PERFECT CAREER

I AM OPEN TO LET MY DIVINE PLAN REVEAL ITSELF TO ME NOW

I AM OPEN TO MY PERFECT LOVING PARTNER NOW

I AM READY TO RECEIVE MY GOOD

I AM OPEN ONLY TO TRUTH

I AM COURAGE

I AM WISDOM

I AM WHOLE

I AM PROVIDING GOOD IN THE WORLD

I AM LOVING GOD

I AM LOVING MYSELF

I AM MAKING PEACE WITH MY ENEMIES

I AM ALLOWING GOOD IN ALL PHASES OF MY LIFE

Get the picture. Affirm out loud at least 15 minutes a day. And then be open to letting God provide and you tell no one of your plans – only those who can see them succeed. There is tremendous power in words and thoughts.

So be it and Selah,
Sananda

For workshop information,
write to:

Denise R. Cooney
596 Elm Avenue
Saddlebrook, N. J. 07662
U.S.A.